favourite Recipes from
THE CAPTAIN'S TABLE

Compiled by Simon Haseltine

Illustrated with vintage postcards

SALMON

FAVOURITE CAPTAIN'S TABLE RECIPES

Elegant cruise ships and grand ocean liners have provided a luxurious and fashionable way to travel the world, see the sights and taste some truly sumptuous food. Although not everyone would have been eligible to eat at the Captain's Table, all first class passengers would have enjoyed a bountiful breakfast to start their day at sea, followed by an opulent 4-course luncheon, and the day finishing with an extravagant 8-course dinner. This book samples a day in the life on the high seas over the last 100 years and brings together a selection of recipes to compliment any dining table.

MENU

DINNER

SS *Nieuw Amsterdam* by Bernard W. Church

YARMOUTH BLOATERS

A very traditional British breakfast dish to remind passengers of a taste from home...

For each serving: **1 Yarmouth bloater** **1 tomato** **Knob butter** **Chives (chopped)**

Cut the tomato in half and remove the head and tail from the Yarmouth bloater. Split the fish down the back and open it out flat. Place the tomato and fish under a hot grill and cook on both sides for 5 minutes until lightly browned. Arrange the fish and tomato halves on a serving plate, garnish with a pat of butter and sprinkle with the chopped chives.

SALMON FISHCAKES SERVED WITH A TOMATO SAUCE

Breakfast on board RMS Queen Mary was equally an elegant meal compared to luncheon or dinner, with an overwhelming choice of tempting dishes to start your day at sea...

Fishcakes: 1 lb. potatoes (cubed)   12 oz. salmon fillet   2 tsp. tomato ketchup   1 tsp. English mustard   ½ lemon (zest)
1 tbsp. parsley (chopped)   1 tbsp. dill (chopped)   3 tbsp. plain flour   1 egg (beaten)   4 oz. dried breadcrumbs
Salt and pepper (to season)   Oil   1 lemon (cut into wedges to serve)

Pre-heat the grill. Place the potatoes in a saucepan of water, bring to the boil and simmer for 15 minutes or until tender. Drain and mash. Meanwhile, season the salmon and grill for 5 minutes until just cooked. Cool slightly then break into large flakes. Mix together the potato, tomato ketchup, mustard, lemon zest, herbs and season. Fold in the salmon pieces and shape into 4 large patties. Put the flour, egg and breadcrumbs in 3 bowls. Dip the patties into the flour, then the egg and finally coat in the breadcrumbs. Heat the oil in a large pan and fry the salmon cakes for 5 minutes each side until deep golden. Serve with tomato sauce and lemon wedges.
Serves 4

POTAGE CULTIVATEUR

A classic French soup

1 tablespoon butter 2 slices smoked bacon (cut into small pieces) 1 leek (thinly sliced)
Handful green cabbage (thinly shredded) 2 carrots (thinly sliced) 1 small turnips (small cubes) 1 stick celery (thinly sliced)
2½ pints water Salt and pepper (to season) 1 potato (small cubes) Handful green beans (cut into small pieces)
2 oz. peas 2 oz. gruyère cheese (grated) 6 baguette slices (toasted)

In a large stock pot, melt the butter and cook the bacon for five minutes until brown. Add the leek, cabbage, carrots, turnips and celery and sauté for 10 minutes until soft. Add the water, bring to the boil, then gently simmer for 20 minutes. Season with salt and pepper, add the potatoes and simmer for further 15 minutes. Add the green beans and peas and simmer for a final 5 minutes. Serve with gruyère cheese sprinkled over the toasted baguette slices. Serves 4 to 6.

SS NIEUW AMSTERDAM (1907)

OYSTER PATTIES

An impressive American-inspired entrée…

**12 ready-to-bake vol-au-vent puff pastry shells   4 dozen oysters   2 rashers smoked bacon (cut into small pieces)
Knob unsalted butter (softened)   2 fl. oz. cream   1 onion (finely chopped)   1½ oz. plain flour   Handful parsley (shredded)
Pinch ground cayenne   Salt and ground black pepper   4 spring onions (thinly sliced)**

Bake the puff pastry shells according to package directions until golden brown and puffed, then set aside to cool. Shuck the oysters into a bowl to catch the liquid from the shells.

Next, sauté the bacon for 10 minutes until crisp, remove and drain on paper towels. Add a good knob of butter to the bacon fat and sauté the onions or until softened. Stir in the flour and continue cooking for a minute or so until the flour cooked through. Whisk in the oyster juices and cream and cook for a further minute. Next, add the oysters, bacon, parsley, cayenne and seasoning. Turn the heat down and cook for 2 minutes, stirring all the time. Remove from the heat and set aside.

To serve, fill the puff pastry shells with the oyster mixture and garnish each with spring onion. Makes 12 patties.

RMS *Mauretania* by John H. Fry

FRENCH LAMB POT PIE

A classic café-style meat pie

Olive oil   2 lb. lamb shoulder (cubed)   12 shallots (peeled)   4 carrots (small chunks)   8 oz. mushrooms (quartered)
2 heaped tbsp. plain flour   3 pints water   2 cans chopped tomatoes   4 garlic cloves (crushed)   2 fresh thyme sprigs
1 tbsp. rich chicken stock   Salt and freshly ground pepper   Splash of soy sauce   1 red chilli (chopped)   2 bay leaves
1 swede (small cubes)   12 new/salad potatoes (cubed)   2 oz. peas   3 tbsp. parsley (chopped)
1 pack puff pastry sheets (thawed)   1 egg   2 fl. oz. milk

Heat a little oil in a large ovenproof dish and seal the lamb, then remove and set aside. Next, sauté the shallots, chilli, carrots and mushrooms for around 10 minutes until just coloured. Then add the flour, stir and briefly cook. Pour in the water and add the tomatoes, garlic, thyme, stock, seasonings, soy sauce and bay leaves. Stir and bring to the boil. Return the lamb and gently simmer for 30 minutes. Next, add the swede and potatoes, stir and simmer for 30 minutes or until the vegetables are tender. Finally, add the peas and parsley and set aside to cool a little before removing the bay leaves.

Preheat the oven to 200°C/400°F/Gas 6. Cut rounds in the pastry sheets to fit the top of 6 small pie dishes (or you can use one large dish if desired). Next, spoon the lamb mixture into each dish. Beat together the egg and milk and brush the pastry edges with the egg wash. Place a pastry on top of each dish, press down the sides and brush all over with the remaining egg wash. Then bake in the oven for 25 minutes or until golden brown. Serves 6.

ROAST CHICKEN
Served with Bread Sauce and Succotash

A wonderful dish of roast chicken and succotash – an American-inspired side dish of sweetcorn and broad beans seasoned with chilli, basil, mint and garlic…

Roast Chicken: 1 onion (chopped)   2 carrots (chopped)   1 free range chicken (around 3 lb.)   1 lemon (halved)   **Bunch thyme**
Knob butter (softened)   Salt and pepper
For the gravy: 1 tablespoon plain flour   8 fl. oz. chicken stock

Preheat the oven to 190°C/375°F/Gas 5. Place the prepared vegetables on the bottom of a roasting tin. Season the cavity of the chicken and stuff with the lemon halves and thyme. Sit the chicken on the vegetables, baste the breast and legs with the butter, then season with salt and pepper. Place in the oven and bake for 1 hr 30 minutes or until cooked (when the juices run clear). Remove the chicken to rest for 20 minutes. Discard the vegetables but retain all the juices in the roasting tin. While the chicken is resting, make the gravy. Place the roasting tin over a low flame, then stir in the flour and sauté for a few minutes. Gradually pour in the stock, stirring all the time, until the sauce thickens. Strain the gravy into a small saucepan, then simmer and season to taste. Serve the chicken with roast potatoes and succotash.

Succotash: 4 sweetcorn cobs (or 2 large tins sweetcorn, drained)   **Glug olive oil   2 garlic cloves (crushed)**
4 oz. broad beans (shelled)   1 red chilli (chopped)   Large handful basil (chopped)   Large handful mint (chopped)
2 teaspoons sherry vinegar

Use a knife to cut down the length of the sweetcorn to remove the kernels. Heat the oil in a large sauté pan and cook the kernels and garlic over a medium heat for 5 minutes, stirring all the time. Add the broad beans, cover and gently cook for further 5 minutes until the beans are tender. Turn off the heat and fold through the chilli, herbs and vinegar. Season to taste and serve with the roast chicken.   Serves 4.

Eleven

RMS LUSITANIA (1908)

RMMV *Britannic* by John Nicholson

POACHED EGG FLORENTINE

An indulgent light lunch...

For the hollandaise sauce: 4 oz. butter (cubes) 2 egg yolks ½ tbsp cold water ½ tbsp. lemon juice
Salt and freshly ground white pepper
For the eggs Florentine: 2 English muffins (warmed, cut in half, buttered) 2 large handfuls baby spinach (steamed)
4 free-range eggs (poached)

Preheat the grill to medium. For the hollandaise sauce, place half the butter into a small saucepan and melt slowly over a gentle heat, then set aside. Place the egg yolks into a bowl set over a pan of gently simmering water and beat until pale and thickened. Add the water, then beat for another 30 seconds. Add half of the remaining cubes of butter to the egg mixture and stir for a few minutes until the mixture thickens. Remove from the heat and beat in the rest of the cubed butter. Next, pour in the melted butter and whisk until the sauce reaches the consistency of double cream. Season to taste with lemon juice, salt and pepper. Keep the sauce warm by resting the bowl in the pan of warm water.

Place the warm buttered muffins onto a baking tray. Arrange the steamed spinach on top of the muffins, top with the poached eggs and pour the hollandaise sauce over the top. Place the tray under the preheated grill for 2 minutes, or until the top is bubbling and golden brown. Transfer the eggs Florentine onto two serving plates and serve immediately. Serves 2.

NAVARIN – FRENCH LAMB STEW

A delicately cooked lamb stew, named in commemoration of the French naval victory at Navarin in the early 1800s

**2 lb. lamb fillet (shoulder or leg, trimmed – cut into 1 inch cubes) Olive oil 1 onion (chopped)
1 sweet potato (peeled and diced) 2 carrots (chopped) 4 cloves garlic (crushed) 1 tin plum tomatoes
1 tablespoon dried herbes de Provence 8 fl. oz. dry red wine Salt and freshly ground black pepper (to season)
1½ pints lamb stock French bread (to serve)**

Season the meat and fry for 5 minutes until brown. Remove with a slotted spoon and set aside. Next, add the onion, potatoes and carrots and sauté for 5 minutes. Add the garlic and cook for a further minute. Next, add the tomatoes, herbs, red wine and season. Simmer until reduced by half. Add the lamb and stock to the pan and return to a boil. Reduce the heat and gently simmer for about 30 minutes or until the lamb is tender. Ladle into large bowls and serve with chunks of warm crusty French bread.

ROAST SADDLE OF LAMB
Served Garnished with Vegetables

Lunch on board the Royal Yacht was a regal occasion
for HM Queen Elizabeth and her guests

Saddle of young lamb (around 6 lb. in weight)   **2 oz. butter (softened)**   **2 sprigs of fresh rosemary**
Salt and pepper (to season)   **Selection of vegetables (roasted to serve)**

Preheat the oven to 190°C/375°F/Gas 5.   Spread the butter over the joint, place the rosemary on top and season well with salt and pepper. Place in a roasting tin and cover with foil. Roast for 25 minutes to the lb., plus an extra 25 minutes. Remove the foil after the first half hour of cooking time. Lift out the joint and place on a warm serving dish. Serve with roast potatoes and a selection of roasted vegetables, together with a rich homemade gravy. Serves 6.

HMS BRITANNIA (1959)

LENTILS À LA BRETONNE

A very elegant lentil vegetarian lunch dish

14 oz. French green lentils | **3½ pints chicken broth (warm)** | **1 carrot (chopped)** | **1 stick celery (chopped)**
1 onion (chopped) | **Knob butter** | **5 g. flour** | **1 clove garlic (crushed)** | **Salt and pepper (to season)**
Handful fresh parsley (to serve)

Melt the butter in a large stock pot, add the onion and celery and sauté for 5 minutes until the onions are soft. Add the carrot, flour and garlic, cook for a further minute, stirring constantly. Next, add the stock and lentils, season to taste and bring to a boil. Cover partially, reduce the heat and gently simmer for 50 minutes until the lentils are tender. Cool slightly, then purée the soup until the broth is still slightly thick and lumpy. Season with salt and pepper. Garnish with the fresh chopped parsley and serve with chunks of French bread. Serves 4.

RMS *Queen Mary* by John Nicholson

GRILLED SPRING CHICKEN
Served with Sauce Robert

A classic French mustard sauce served with grilled spring chicken for first class lunch

1 spring chicken   **Salt and pepper**   **2 oz. butter for basting (softened)**
Robert Sauce: **1 onion (chopped)**   **Knob butter**   **4 fl. oz. white wine**   **8 fl. oz. rich beef stock**   **1 tablespoon Dijon mustard**
Freshly ground pepper (to season)

Season the inside of the chicken and place onto a rotisserie. Set the grill on high and cook for 10 minutes. Mix together the softened butter with a dash of salt and pepper. Turn the grill down to medium and baste the chicken with the butter mixture. Cook for 1½ hours, basting occasionally, until cooked (check juices run clear). Remove from the rotisserie and let stand for 10 minutes before carving at the table. Serve with the Sauce Robert and a selection of spring vegetables.

Meanwhile, to make the Sauce Robert, sauté the onion in the butter for 5 minutes until translucent. Add the white wine and reduce. Next, add the beef stock, stir and reduce until the sauce is thick enough to coat the back of a spoon. Add the mustard and season to taste. Serves 4.

LOBSTER MAYONNAISE SALAD

For those wanting a lighter lunch, this delicious and refreshing salad is easy to make

1 lb. lobster meat (cooked) 1 cucumber (peeled, seeded and finely diced) 6 oz. mayonnaise
4 spring onions (thinly sliced) Sea salt and freshly ground black pepper

Combine the lobster meat, cucumber and mayonnaise in a large bowl, then fold through the spring onions. Season with salt and pepper, cover and chill for 30 minutes before serving. Serve with chunks of French bread. Serves 6.

RMS *Mauretania* II by Bernard W. Church

CHAMPAGNE JELLY

A bubbly, summery dessert – perfect after an 8-course dinner…

10 fl. oz. hot water   2 oz. caster sugar   16 fl. oz. pink champagne   4 leaves of gelatine
5 oz. raspberries   Whipped Cream (to serve)

Put the hot water and sugar into a small saucepan over medium heat and stir to dissolve the sugar, then bring to a boil. Reduce the heat and simmer for five minutes, then remove the pan. Pour the champagne into a large heatproof bowl and add the gelatine. Set aside for 5 minutes until the leaves are soft. Take out the leaves and add them to the sugar syrup. Whisk until the gelatine has completely dissolved, then pour the syrup back into the bowl with the champagne and whisk to combine. Allow to cool then refrigerate the jelly for about one hour. As soon as it starts to thicken, stir in the raspberries. Divide the jelly between six glasses, cover and refrigerate for six hours until set. Serve with a dollop of whipped cream on top. Serves 6.

RMS MAURETANIA (1907)

SAGO PUDDING

A warming, creamy, buttery luxurious pudding with a hint of spice and topped with fresh fruit and nuts

2 oz. sago   1½ pints milk   2 tablespoons sugar   ½ oz. butter (plus extra for greasing)   Pinch freshly grated nutmeg
***Topping:* Selection fresh fruit and chopped nuts.**

Gently heat the milk in a heavy-based saucepan until warm, then gradually sprinkle in the sago, stirring all the time. Next, add the sugar and butter and bring to a simmer. Cook for 10 minutes, stirring frequently until the pudding has thickened. Preheat the oven to 180°C/350°F/Gas 4. Pour the sago pudding into a buttered ovenproof dish (around 2 pint capacity), and grate the nutmeg over the top. Bake in the oven for 30 minutes. Serve hot or cold, topped with fresh fruit and nuts.   Serves 4.

HORS D'OEUVRES

Mingling with your fellow passengers, savouring a delicious selection of posh nibbles...

Selection to serve 6
ANCHOVIES ON TOAST
4 slices white bread   **Glug olive oil**   **Knob butter (softened)**   **1 tin anchovies**   **Handful fresh basil (shredded)**

To toast the bread, brush a large baking sheet with olive oil. Brush both sides of the bread with olive oil, place on the baking tray and grill for 10 minutes, turning once, until toasted. Remove from the grill and allow to cool. Butter the toast, then cut it into fingers the same size as the anchovies. Drain the anchovies and lay an anchovy on each finger of toast. Sprinkle with a few shredded basil leaves and serve immediately.

RUSSIAN CAVIAR

Medallions of venison served with a classic French peppery sauce

I tin Russian caviar **3 eggs (hard boiled)** **1 lemon (cut into wedges)** **1 red onion (thinly diced)** **Bunch chives (chopped)**
4 fl. oz. crème fraîche **4 slices white bread** **Olive oil**

To toast the bread, brush a large baking sheet with olive oil. Brush both sides of the bread with olive oil, place on the baking tray and grill for 10 minutes, turning once, until toasted. Remove from the grill and allow cooling before cutting into triangles. Peel the eggs and separate the whites and yolks. Chop the yolks and whites and place in 2 small separate bowls and sprinkle with the chives. Next, spoon the caviar into a small decorative bowl. To serve, place the caviar bowl in the centre of a large platter and surround with small bowls of chopped egg yolks and egg whites, lemon wedges, red onion, crème fraîche and the triangles of toast. Serve immediately.

SS *Stratheden* by Bernard W. Church

CREVETTE COCKTAIL

A classic prawn cocktail...

**12 oz. prawns (cooked, shells on) 2 little gem lettuces 6 tablespoons mayonnaise
2 tablespoons tomato ketchup (good quality brand) 2 teaspoons Worcestershire sauce 2 teaspoons horseradish sauce
Splash tabasco sauce Lemon juice (a squeeze) Bunch chives (snipped) Black pepper Paprika (to dust)
Brown bread and butter (to serve)**

Peel all the prawns except 4 and set these aside. Shred the lettuce and divide evenly between 4 glass dishes.
Place the peeled prawns on the lettuce and season with a little black pepper. Mix together the mayonnaise,
tomato ketchup, Worcestershire sauce, horseradish sauce and a splash of tabasco, then add a squeeze of lemon
juice and stir well. Spoon over the prawns, dust with a little paprika and sprinkle over the chopped chives.
Serve with triangles of brown bread and butter. Serves 4.

SWEETBREAD PATTIES
Served with a Périgueux Sauce

Périgueux is a rich brown sauce flavoured with Madeira from the Périgord region of South-west France, famous for truffles

8 oz. sweetbreads   ½ pint chicken stock   1 egg (beaten)   8 oz. breadcrumbs   Salad garnish
Périgueux sauce: 2 fl. oz. demi-glacé stock (or a homemade beef stock, reduced)   2 small cans truffles (minced)
1 tablespoon of the liquid from the tinned truffles   Splash Madeira   Knob unsalted butter   Salt and pepper to season

Rinse, then soak the sweetbreads in cold water overnight in the fridge, changing the water a few times. The next day, bring the chicken stock to the boil and gently poach the sweetbreads for around 15 minutes, then drain and allow to cool. When cold, peel away the skins, dip into the beaten egg and then the breadcrumbs and fry in a little oil for 5 minutes to brown on both sides.

Meanwhile to make the Périgueux sauce, simmer the stock over a low heat and add the minced truffles, a little liquid from the tin, a good splash of Madeira and gently simmer for 2 minutes, then remove from the heat. Whisk in the butter and season to taste.

Serve the sweetbreads topped with the Périgueux sauce and a salad garnish.   Serves 4.

RMS MAURETANIA (1934)

SS *Canton* by Bernard W. Church

PETITE MARMITE

Marmite is French for a "little pot" – here is a recipe for a delicious meat and vegetable soup….

6 oz. veal (sliced) 1 lb. beef short ribs 1 onion (chopped – skin on) 1 clove garlic 2 pints beef stock
4 fl. oz. red wine Pinch salt Pinch dried mixed herbs 1 bay leaf 4 peppercorns Small bunch parsley (shredded)
Knob unsalted butter 1 leek (chopped) 1 carrot (chopped) 1 stalk celery (chopped)
Handful cabbage leaves (finely shredded) Salt and freshly ground pepper to season

In a large stock pan, place the veal, ribs, onion, garlic, peppercorns, parsley, bay leaf, beef stock, wine, dried herbs and a pinch of salt. Cover and simmer gently for 2 hours until the meat is tender. Skim off any scum and remove the meat from the pot and set aside to cool. Remove and discard the bones and shred the meat into small bite-size pieces. Strain the stock, discard the solids, and set aside. In a second large stock pot, melt the butter and add the leek, carrot and celery and sauté for 5 minutes until softened. Next, add the meat and stock, bring to a boil, then simmer for 30 minutes, adding the cabbage with 10 minutes to go. Season well and serve in warm bowls. Serves 4.

MARASCHINO SORBET

A tangy cherry sorbet to cleanse the palate between courses

1 jar maraschino cherries (around 16 oz.)   4 fl. oz. juice from the cherries (top up with water)   1 tablespoon caster sugar

If required, stone the cherries. Purée the cherries, juice and sugar in a blender until smooth and then strain through a sieve. Discard the solids and chill the juice for a few hours. Process in an ice-cream maker in accordance the manufacturer's instructions. Freeze until ready to use and serve with some sweetened whipped cream. Serves 4.

FILET OF SOLE
Served with Lobster Butter and Shoe-string Fries

On Independence Day, passengers sitting at Captain Lt-Commander Anderson's table enjoyed this delicious dish...

Sole: Serves 4   **4 filets of sole (skinned)**   **4 large knobs butter (to fry)**
Lobster butter: **Handful lobster shells**   **4 oz. unsalted butter**   **Small splash Pernod**

To make the lobster butter, dry the lobster shells in the oven for 30 minutes, then crush into small pieces with a rolling pin. Melt the butter in a bowl placed over a pan of simmering water, add Pernod and the shell pieces and continue to heat gently for 10 minutes. Set aside for 30 minutes then strain through a very fine mesh to remove all the shell. Cool the butter and refrigerate. Once cold, shape into 4 patties.

Heat the remaining butter in a large pan and fry the sole for around 2 minutes on each side until cooked through, basting with the butter all the time. Serve hot topped with the lobster butter patties, a salad garnish and a handful of shoe-string fries.

Shoe-string fries: Serves 4   **2 potatoes (peeled)**   **Salt and pepper for seasoning**   **Olive oil**

Preheat the oven to 220°C/425°F/Gas 7 and lightly coat a baking tray with a little olive oil. Cut the potatoes into "shoe-strings" using a mandolin cutter, then pat dry with a kitchen towel. In a bowl, toss together the potato, a glug of olive oil and a good pinch of salt until well coated. Spread evenly on the baking tray and bake in the oven for 20 minutes, turning the potatoes a few times, until golden brown all over. Season with a little salt and serve.

SS ALEUTIAN (1935)

ROAST DUCKLING
Served with a Rich Port Dressing and Apple Sauce

Dining in style ensured your cruise sailed by in an elegant fashion with a chance to catch up with the fashionable gossip...

Main

1 large duck, with giblets   Fine sea salt

Preheated the oven to 220°C/425°F/Gas 7. Remove the giblets and prick the skin around the duck legs. Season with salt and place on a rack in a roasting tin and roast in the middle of the oven for 20 minutes per 1 lb. plus 25 minutes extra. When the duck is cooked (check juices run clear), remove from the oven, loosely cover with foil and rest for 20 minutes before serving. Serve with port gravy, apple sauce, roast potatoes and seasonal vegetables.

Port gravy: **2 teaspoons vegetable oil   Giblets from the duck   1 onion (chopped)   1 celery (chopped)   1 carrot (chopped)
Salt and pepper (to season)   1 bay leaf   Pinch mixed herbs   2 tablespoons flour   8 fl. oz. tawny port   8 fl. oz. water**

In a large saucepan fry the giblets in the oil for a few minutes until brown all over. Add the onion, celery, carrot, bay leaf, herbs and seasoning and sauté for 5 minutes until softened. Add the flour and cook through. Add the port and simmer gently for 5 minutes. Finally, add the water and simmer for 1 hour until reduced (add a little extra water if required). Remove from the heat and strain, ready to serve. Serves 4.

RMS *Queen Elizabeth* by Bernard W. Church

GRENADINE OF VENISON
Served with Poivrade Sauce

Medallions of venison served with a classic French peppery sauce

8 medallions of venison (from the loin)   Knob butter   2 fl. oz. chicken stock   ½ fl. oz. grenadine
Salt and pepper (to season)   6 fl. oz. poivrade sauce (see recipe)
Poivrade sauce: ½ bottle red wine   Splash red wine vinegar   1 onion (diced)   1 carrot (diced)   1 stalk celery (diced)
1 clove garlic (chopped)   1 small bunch thyme   1 bay leaf   4 juniper berries   ½ teaspoon black peppercorns
7 oz. granulated sugar   Splash double cream   Olive oil

Season the venison with a little salt and pepper and heat the butter in a frying pan. Sauté the venison for 3 minutes each side until cooked medium-rare, adding a few more minutes for medium, or as desired. Remove from the pan and set aside to keep warm. Deglaze the sauté pan with the chicken stock and simmer until reduced by half. Add the Poivrade Sauce and Grenadine to the pan and simmer for a few minutes. To serve, spoon the sauce over the venison and serve with seasonal vegetables.

Meanwhile, to make the poivrade sauce: In a bowl add the wine, vinegar, onion, carrot, celery, garlic, thyme, bay leaf, peppercorns and juniper berries and marinade for a few hours. Strain the marinade into a bowl, reserving the vegetables. Heat the oil in a pan, add the vegetables and sauté for 10 minutes until brown, then add the sugar and cook for a few more minutes until caramelised. Next, pour in the marinade, stir and simmer for 30 minutes to reduce the sauce by two-thirds, skimming the surface as required. Strain into a saucepan and simmer until a coating consistency is achieved. Skim, then add the cream to finish the sauce. Serves 4

MARROW FARCI

A delicious vegetarian dish to serve your own first class diners...

1 marrow   Glug olive oil   2 red onions (finely chopped)   4 cloves garlic (crushed)   Bunch fresh basil (chopped)
1 teaspoon mixed herbs   1 teaspoon tomato purée   6 oz. button mushrooms (chopped)   2 tablespoons red wine vinegar
6 oz. cooked rice   Salt and pepper   2 oz. mature Cheddar cheese (grated)   ½ oz. fresh bread crumbs
Large knob butter (melted)   Handful fresh basil (for garnish)

Preheat the oven to 180°C/350°F/Gas 4. Halve the marrow lengthwise and scoop out all the flesh and seeds. Discard the seeds and chop the flesh into small chunks. Sauté the onions and garlic in the oil for 10 minutes until softened and lightly browned. Next, stir in basil, mixed herbs, marrow chunks and tomato purée and gently cook for 5 minutes. Add the mushrooms and cook for a further 5 minutes, then stir in the vinegar and remove from the heat to cool. Stir in the rice and half the cheese and season to taste. Spoon the mixture into the hollowed marrow shell, sprinkle with the bread crumbs and remaining cheese and drizzle with melted butter. Place in a greased baking dish and bake for 40 minutes or until marrow is tender and topping is well browned. To serve, slice the marrow into 6 equal portions and garnish with fresh basil. Serves 6.

RMS *Orion* by Bernard W. Church

JOCKEY CLUB SALAD

Passengers dined on the decadent Jockey Club Salad which was created by the great chef Escoffier in New York

2 small black truffles (wiped clean)   8 oz. cooked chicken (sliced)   ½ bunch asparagus (trimmed and halved)
½ lettuce (shredded)   A little white wine   French salad dressing

First, poach the truffles in a little white wine for 5 minutes, then remove from the pan and cool. At the same time, steam the asparagus spears for around 2 minutes, then remove and allow to cool. Arrange the lettuce in the serving bowl and fold through the chicken pieces and asparagus. Shave the truffles over the salad and gently toss together. Cover with a French salad dressing and serve. Serves 4.

PLUM PUDDING
Served with a Brandy and Hard Sauce

During the early 20th century, plum pudding was served all year round with a delicious, rich and sweet "hard sauce"

1 homemade or shop bought Christmas pudding
Hard sauce: **4 oz. unsalted butter (softened)   7 oz. sugar   1 teaspoon vanilla extract   Good splash brandy**

Beat butter in a mixer until fluffy. Next, gradually add the sugar, then the vanilla extract and brandy and beat until smooth. Serve at room temperature, dolloped over a steaming hot plum pudding. Serves 4.

POUDING DIPLOMATIC

The most diplomatic of all puddings served as part of an eight-course dinner menu

1 pint milk   3 eggs   4 oz. sugar   3 oz. candied fruit (diced)   1 teaspoon kirsch
1 packet sponge boudoir biscuits (snapped into cubes)   Whipped cream (sweetened, to serve)

Preheat the oven to 170°C/325°F/Gas 3. In a mixing bowl, whisk the eggs and sugar together. In a heavy-based saucepan, bring the milk to a boil. Pour the hot milk over the egg mixture and stir well until thick, then strain. In a small bowl, combine the candied fruit and kirsch and let stand for a few minutes. Line the bottom of a charlotte mould with wax paper. Cover with the candied fruit, then add the biscuits to fill the mould. Pour over the thick custard and bake in water bath for 1 hour until set. Cool completely before removing from the mould to a serving dish. Serve with sweetened whipped cream. Serves 8.

SS ALBERTIC (1930)

PEACHES IN CHARTREUSE JELLY

Chartreuse is a sweet, spicy, pungent liqueur dating back to the Carthusian monks since 1737

5 teaspoons powdered gelatine **8 fl. oz. water (to dissolve the gelatine)** **8 fl. oz. water (to make the jelly)**
2½ oz. caster sugar **8 fl. oz. Chartreuse French liqueur** **2 large peaches (peeled and sliced)** **14 oz. granulated sugar**
1 pint water (to poach peaches) **1 lemon (juice)** **1 cinnamon stick** **2 cloves** **Sprig of mint to garnish**

Line a glass dish with cling film. Dissolve the gelatine powder in the water for 5 minutes. Meanwhile, make the jelly by bringing 8 fl. oz. water to a boil in a saucepan, reduce the heat and stir in the caster sugar until dissolved. Remove from the heat and add the Chartreuse liqueur and gelatine mixture and stir well to combine. Pour into the lined dish and leave for in a cool place for 2 hours to set. Next, to poach the peaches, add the granulated sugar to 1 pint of water in a saucepan, heat and stir until the sugar is dissolved. Bring to a boil and simmer for a minute until the syrup is clear. Add the lemon juice, cinnamon stick and cloves and stir, then add the peaches and poach in the syrup for 5 minutes. Remove from the heat and allow to cool in the pan. When cold, lift the jelly out of the baking dish and cut into small squares. To serve, place the poached peaches in glass dishes and top with the jelly cubes and a sprig of mint. Serves 4.

RMS *Titanic* by John H. Fry

Pudding

FRENCH CUSTARD PIE

A delicious Parisian flan filled with an egg vanilla custard

Makes an 8 inch flan
8 inch flan pastry (chilled)   **1½ pints milk**   **9 oz. sugar**   **1 vanilla pod (split and scraped)**   **6 tablespoons cornflour**
8 fl. oz. double cream   **4 egg yolks**   **1 egg**

In a large saucepan bring the milk, sugar, vanilla pod and seeds to the boil, then remove from the heat, cover and leave for 10 minutes. Meanwhile, mix the cornflour with the cream into a paste, then whisk in the egg yolks and whole egg. Next, gradually stir in the infused milk and cook over a low heat, stirring all the time, until the custard thickens. Remove from heat, strain and cool. Preheat the oven to 200°C/400°F/Gas 6. Line a flan tin with the pastry, pour in the cool custard and bake 45 minutes until the custard is slightly wobbly. Increase the temperature of the oven to its highest and bake for a further 5 minutes. Remove and cool before refrigerating for 6 hours to fully set. Serve with a dollop of whipped cream.

SS ALEUTIAN (1935)

CHARLOTTE RUSSE

A classic rich Bavarian cream-filled pudding, dating back to the early 19th century...

1 pint orange jelly (made up but kept warm so as not to set)   **1 packet sponge boudoir biscuits**   **½ pint double cream**
1 heaped tablespoon icing sugar   **1 teaspoon vanilla extract**   **Glug sherry**   **2 bananas** (mashed)
1 lb. strawberries and raspberries and blueberries (in total)   **6 glacé cherries to decorate**   **Extra whipped cream to decorate**

Line the base of a spring-form cake tin with cling film. Pour around half the jelly over the bottom and allow to set, then cover with the fresh fruit pieces. Meanwhile, whip the cream with the icing sugar and add the vanilla extract until thick and peaky. In a separate bowl, combine the mashed banana and remaining jelly and whisk together, then fold into the cream. Line the edge of the cake tin with the sponge biscuits and sprinkle with a little sherry. Now, dollop the cream and jelly mixture into the middle, covering the fruit. Set in the fridge for 4 hours before turning out onto a serving plate, by carefully running a knife around the edge. Decorate with glacé cherries and serve with another dollop of whipped cream.

SS CITY OF ROME (1900)

Forty-Three

QSMV *Dominion Monarch* by Bernard W. Church

VIENNA PUDDING
Served with Pistachio Sauce
A delicious pudding with a wonderful nutty pistachio sauce…

Vienna pudding: **4 slices stale white bread (small chunks) 3 oz. sultanas 5 fl. oz. sherry 4 oz. light brown sugar 2 oz. chopped mixed peel 1 lemon (finely grated rind) 3 eggs ½ pint milk Knob butter (for greasing)**
Pistachio sauce: **4 oz. roasted pistachio nuts (shelled and skinned) 7 oz. sugar 1 egg white 1 pint milk 4 egg yolks**

To make the pudding, place the chunks of bread, sultanas and sherry in a bowl, mix well and leave to soak for 30 minutes, then beat with a fork to break up. Next, add the sugar, mixed peel and lemon rind. Beat the eggs and milk together and mix into the bread mixture. Dollop into a well-buttered pudding basin, cover with a double thickness of greased greaseproof paper and tie under the rim to secure. Steam for 2 hours. Serve with pistachio sauce.

To make the pistachio sauce, place the nuts in a food processor and whizz until ground. Add half the sugar and the egg white and whizz until the mixture forms a paste. Spoon the pistachio paste into a saucepan, add the milk and bring the mixture to a boil. Remove from the heat, cool for 5 minutes, then strain through a fine-mesh sieve into another saucepan and set aside. Whisk together the egg yolks and the remaining sugar until thick and light. Whisk in half the strained milk, then whisk the mixture back into the remaining milk. Cook the sauce over low heat, stirring constantly, until thick enough to coat the back of a spoon. Cool and refrigerate for 24 hours before serving. Serves 4

MS MILWAUKEE (1937)

RMMV *Athlone Castle* by Bernard W. Church

FRENCH ICE CREAM

A rich, creamy traditional French ice cream…

Makes 2 pints

6 eggs yolks   4 oz. sugar   14 fl .oz. double cream   10 fl. oz. milk   1 vanilla pod (split in half lengthways)   Pinch salt

In a bowl, beat together the egg yolks and half the sugar until smooth and creamy. Next, pour the cream, most of the milk, the remaining sugar and a pinch of salt into a large saucepan. Scrape out the vanilla seeds and add to the pan, then heat gently until the mixture is steaming, whisking all the time. Remove from the heat to allow the vanilla to infuse for 5 minutes. Now, gradually whisk the hot cream into the egg yolks. Pour the mixture into a clean saucepan and gently heat for around 5 minutes, stirring all the time until the custard thickens. Remove from the heat and stir through the remaining milk. Next, sieve the custard into a bowl and cool, stirring frequently. Then refrigerate the custard until completely cold. Pour the custard into an ice-cream machine and follow the manufacturer's instructions. Serve with wafers.

METRIC CONVERSIONS

The weights, measures and oven temperatures used in the preceding recipes can be easily converted to their metric equivalents. The conversions listed below are only approximate, having been rounded up or down as may be appropriate.

Weights

Avoirdupois	Metric
1 oz.	just under 30 grams
4 oz. (¼ lb.)	app. 115 grams
8 oz. (½ lb.)	app. 230 grams
1 lb.	454 grams

Liquid Measures

Imperial	Metric
1 tablespoon (liquid only)	20 millilitres
1 fl. oz.	app. 30 millilitres
1 gill (¼ pt.)	app. 145 millilitres
½ pt.	app. 285 millilitres
1 pt.	app. 570 millilitres
1 qt.	app. 1,140 litres

Oven Temperatures

	°Fahrenheit	Gas Mark	°Celsius
Slow	300	2	150
	325	3	170
Moderate	350	4	180
	375	5	190
	400	6	200
Hot	425	7	220
	450	8	230
	475	9	240

Flour as specified in these recipes refers to plain flour unless otherwise described.

Title page illustration: Arandora Star by Bernard W. Church